FALCONS IN THE CITY
THE STORY OF A PEREGRINE FAMILY

FALCONS IN THE CITY
THE STORY OF A PEREGRINE FAMILY

TEXT BY CHRIS EARLEY
PHOTOGRAPHY BY LUKE MASSEY

FIREFLY BOOKS

A FIREFLY BOOK

Published by Firefly Books Ltd. 2016

First printing

Publisher Cataloging-in-Publication Data (U.S.)
Names: Earley, Chris G., 1968-, author. | Massey, Luke, photographer.
Title: Falcons in the city : the story of a peregrine family / text by Chris Earley, photography by Luke Massey.
Description: Richmond Hill, Ontario, Canada : Firefly Books, 2016. | Includes index. | Summary: "This book tells the story of a nest of wild birds that choose to lay their eggs high atop a Chicago condominium balcony and the alarm, then charm, of their city landlords... This book explains issues related to urban wildlife and how urban dwellers co-exist with an ever-increasing wildlife population" – Provided by publisher.
Identifiers: ISBN 978-1-77085-804-6 (hardcover) | 978-1-77085-803-9 (paperback)
Subjects: LCSH: Peregrine falcon – United States – Juvenile literature. | Urban animals – Juvenile literature. | Human-animal relationships – Juvenile literature.
Classification: LCC QL696.F34E275 |DDC 598.96 – dc23

Library and Archives Canada Cataloguing in Publication
A CIP record for this title is available from Library and Archives Canada.

Published in the United States by
Firefly Books (U.S.) Inc.
P.O. Box 1338, Ellicott Station
Buffalo, New York 14205

Published in Canada by
Firefly Books Ltd.
50 Staples Avenue, Unit 1
Richmond Hill, Ontario L4B 0A7

Cover and interior design by Gareth Lind, LINDdesign

Printed in China

The publisher gratefully acknowledges the financial support for our publishing program by the Government of Canada through the Canada Book Fund as administered by the Department of Canadian Heritage.

CONTENTS

DISCOVERY

Imagine coming home to your 28th-floor apartment and finding a large bird looking at you through your balcony window. That is what happened to Chicago resident Dacey Arashiba. A peregrine falcon sat on his balcony railing for a few days and then, even more surprising, another one showed up: two peregrine falcons! This was the beginning of Dacey's amazing adventure with his two new neighbors.

Peregrine falcons make messy neighbors. Their nests are usually surrounded by poop and leftover meals, so many people wouldn't want to have these birds living on their balconies. However, because peregrines were considered to be an endangered species for many years, these birds are protected under the Endangered Species Act. This means that people are not allowed to interfere with the birds' activities and nest sites.

When peregrine falcons were still considered endangered, people helped increase their numbers by hatching eggs that were laid by captive adult peregrines and placing the resulting chicks in nests on the sides of buildings. The chicks were fed in a way that they were not able to see the humans who were feeding them and, when the chicks grew up, they left their nests to hunt on their own. Today many peregrine falcons nest in cities, as well as in more natural sites.

IDENTIFICATION

◄ When peregrine falcons fly, you can easily see their long pointed wings.

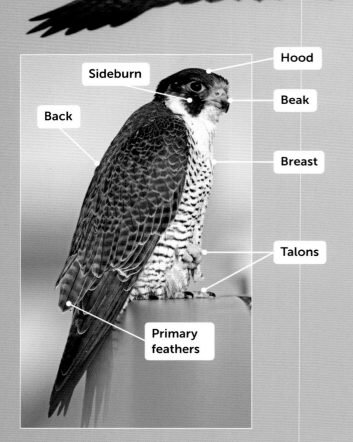

Hood

Sideburn

Beak

Back

Breast

Talons

Primary feathers

Dacey identified his new neighbors by looking for field marks, which are the spots, stripes and patterns that make each bird species unique. Adult peregrine falcons have dark steel-gray backs and wings that are covered in dark bars. Their breasts are whitish with dark spots. The birds have dark hoods with sideburns on the sides of their faces. They also have yellow around their eyes, at the base of their beaks and on their feet. They have long pointed wings and long tails. Their curved beaks and sharp talons show that they are raptors or birds of prey, which means they hunt and feed on other animals. Other raptors include hawks, eagles, ospreys and owls.

There are other raptors that look similar to peregrine falcons. Can you see the differences between these birds and Dacey's neighbor on page 8?

Merlin

This falcon is a relative of the peregrine falcon, but is a much smaller bird. Note that it is missing the peregrine falcon's dark hood and sideburns. Merlins have streaks on their breasts instead of spots.

American kestrel

This is another small falcon species. The male American kestrel has bright rufous or reddish brown coloration on its head, back and tail that peregrine falcons do not have. Can you see other differences?

Cooper's hawk

The adult Cooper's hawk has red eyes and rusty bars on its breast.

Red-tailed hawk

The adult red-tailed hawk is known for its red tail. It does not have the peregrine falcon's dark hood.

FLIGHT

As Dacey was about to learn, peregrine falcons are true masters of the sky. Whether they are flying among the high-rise buildings of a city, above the cliffs of the Arctic landscape or over the beaches on the coast, they are the fastest of the fast. They can also land gently on a balcony railing, float high above us with barely a flap of a wing and maneuver deftly between tall buildings.

◄ One of the peregrine falcons gliding by Dacey's balcony.

Birds can change the shapes of their wings by arranging them into different positions. Peregrine falcons have three main flight patterns: soaring, gliding and stooping.

Soaring

Peregrines and other raptors are good at catching rising currents of warm air called thermals. To use these currents to their maximum potential, the birds spread open their tails and stretch their wings out as far as they can. When most raptors do this, their wings' primary feathers spread apart like fingers. Peregrine falcons' wings are so pointed (an adaptation for extreme speed) that they keep a sharp shape even when the birds are soaring. When peregrines are soaring, they often don't need to flap their wings to stay aloft.

Gliding

For this wing position, the peregrine brings its primary feathers together so they are even more pointed. This allows the bird to cut through the air and go quickly. They often alternate flapping and gliding to fly across the sky very fast.

Stooping

Stooping is the peregrine's specialty. The bird begins stooping by flying high in the air and then it tucks in its wings entirely and drops. It can still control its direction with small wing movements. In this position, peregrines become the fastest animals on earth—they can go over 200 miles per hour! That's over twice as fast as the cars on the highway.

A peregrine in a stoop.

A young peregrine soaring.

◀ A soaring turkey vulture spreads its primary feathers.

11

COURTSHIP

The two peregrines on Dacey's balcony were likely a male and a female. Dacey is a musician, so he decided to name the birds Steve Perry and Linda Perry after the lead singers of two different bands. He thought that the last name "Perry" was very similar to the word "peregrine."

Even though peregrine pairs do not necessarily stick together year-round, they do return to the same nesting area each year, so they have lifelong breeding partnerships.

Courting peregrines renew their pair status with many courtship displays, including head bowing and an exaggerated high-stepping walk known as the "tiptoe walk."

The birds perform courtship displays in the air, as well, including a food transfer where the female receives a food gift from the male. They use special courtship sounds at this time, too, such as "eechip" and "waik" calls.

The female also makes repetitive whining "kree" calls when she is begging for food from the male.

◄ Linda (on the right) calls to her mate, Steve.

13

▲ Steve in the flower-box nest.

NEST

Historically, peregrine falcons nested on cliff-face ledges of mountains, canyons and escarpments. Today, the birds have adapted to a whole new environment: cities. Big, tall buildings have features that peregrines like, such as high lookout points where they can watch for prey and deter predators and flat places where they can lay their eggs. Peregrines don't actually build nests like many birds do. Instead they just lay their eggs in a shallow depression they scrape in the dirt. Linda and Steve decided to nest right inside one of Dacey's balcony flower boxes!

A raptor's nest is also known as an "aerie." Aeries may be used by many different large bird species for decades at a time, and sometimes peregrines use nests that previously belonged to ravens, hawks or eagles.

Often, the white markings of the accumulating bird poop around a nest can be seen from a long distance away.

Peregrines usually have more than one nest site and rotate from one to the other every year. They only raise one brood of chicks each year.

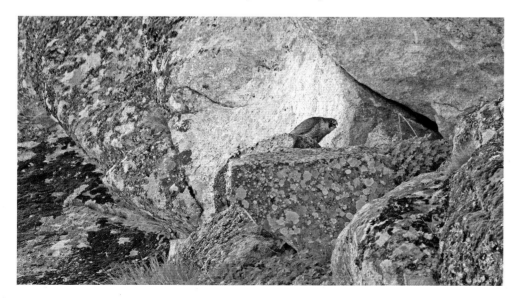

◄ A peregrine falcon at its cliff nest site.

▲ Steve and two of the four eggs.

EGGS

Eggs crushed due to DDT

Imagine how excited Dacey was when he came home one day and found that Linda had laid an egg. Soon she laid another one—and then another and then another. Four eggs! Linda and Steve were going to be very busy parents because caring for eggs takes a lot of work. It takes over a month for the eggs to hatch and the eggs must always be protected by one of the parents' bodies, otherwise the chicks could die of exposure by getting too cold or wet.

When it is first laid, the inside of a peregrine egg looks very similar to the inside of the chicken eggs that we eat. However, a peregrine egg has a fertilized embryo in it that will become a chick. The yellow yolk nourishes the developing chick, while the egg white provides it with water, protein and minerals. The eggshell protects the chick: it stops it from drying out, prevents infection and provides calcium.

Unfortunately, if peregrines ingest certain pesticides, like DDT, the shells of the eggs they produce may be too thin. If this is the case, the eggs may break and the chicks may die. DDT was used from 1946 to 1972 in North America and is one of the main reasons that peregrine falcons became endangered. When DDT was banned, peregrines slowly started to recover, helped by conservation organizations that released young peregrines into cities to increase their numbers.

Both parents sit on the eggs during the incubation period. This is known as brooding. Here Steve broods the eggs, while Linda watches nearby.

Linda defending her nest.

NEST DEFENSE

Raptors are known to fiercely protect their nest sites, and peregrine falcons are no exception. With their impressive flying abilities and sharp talons, peregrines can do serious damage to a potential predator, such as a raccoon or an arctic fox. Peregrine parents have been known to drive away eagles, snowy owls, gyrfalcons, ravens and hawks that threaten their nests.

Once, when a friend and I were checking a nest on an Arctic cliff in Nunavut in northern Canada, I watched a peregrine repeatedly fly at my friend. When the bird pulled up at the bottom of one of its dives it dropped a rock from its talons, firing it at my friend. The falcon then landed on the cliff, where it picked up another rock. When it dived at my friend again, it fired the rock—this time accurately enough to hit his finger!

Witnessing tool-use in birds is very rare. Our encounter shows that anyone can still make important discoveries about peregrine falcons.

Does this look like something you would want to mess with? Linda and Steve, like other peregrine falcons, were very defensive about their nest. Peregrines won't let anything that might harm their eggs or young get too close. Luckily for Dacey, Linda and Steve were very used to humans and seemed to know that he wasn't a threat.

Peregrine Falcon, defending its nest area, gives chase to a Bald Eagle.

◀ The first egg starting to hatch!

◀ The first chick just one hour after hatching.

HATCHING

Happy Hatch Day! Just over a month after the eggs were laid, it was time for Linda and Steve's chicks to arrive. When peregrine chicks hatch, they are covered in fluffy white down and are completely helpless.

Animals that develop in shelled eggs, such as birds and reptiles, need to be able to get past the hard covering of the shell to hatch. How do they do it? Many of these animals have an egg tooth, a small projection on their beak or snout that allows them to break open the shell. Once the animal has hatched, the egg tooth usually disappears after a few days.

Can you see the small white egg tooth under this baby snapping turtle's nose?

This baby great horned owl has an egg tooth on its beak.

▲ Katie, Joe, Luke and Refrigerator.

NESTLING

After all four eggs hatched, Dacey decided to name the chicks after other famous Perrys: Katie (the singer), Luke (the actor), Joe (the guitarist) and Refrigerator (the football player). Even though the chicks weren't in their eggs anymore, Linda and Steve still had to protect the brood from cold temperatures, bad weather and potential predators—but now they also had to feed them. To do that, Linda and Steve needed to hunt more often than before.

▶ The different sizes of these great grey owl chicks show that they hatched at different times.

▲ Steve chasing down a rock pigeon over a busy city street.

HUNTING

A peregrine chasing down a rock pigeon

Peregrines may catch their bird prey by simply flying quickly and seizing them. They tend to hunt in the early morning and late evening, but there are also some records of the birds hunting at night.

Peregrine falcons are fast, but it takes more than speed for them to catch their prey. To hunt efficiently, peregrines must determine the best places to find certain prey species, the best perches to watch for prey, the best ways to take their prey by surprise and the best strategies to catch each prey species. By learning and remembering these tactics, they will be able to catch enough food to raise their growing families.

Peregrines use many different strategies to catch their prey. By stooping, a peregrine can dive down at an incredible speed and hit its target with its talons with such force that the prey is often killed instantly. If the prey doesn't die right away, the peregrine will bite its neck to sever its spinal cord and kill it. Falcons and some other birds of prey have a special projection on their beak called a tomial tooth, which helps them do this. This extra point helps them reach the spot in the neck that will kill their prey most quickly.

Tomial tooth

◄ Like their name suggests, chimney swifts are fast flyers, but they're not fast enough to escape Dacey's peregrines.

PREY

Peregrines mostly eat other birds. Linda and Steve fed mostly on rock pigeons, but they also caught smaller birds, such as red-winged blackbirds and chimney swifts.

Unlike many other raptor species, peregrines rarely catch small mammals (though they do hunt flying bats). Instead, peregrines eat a variety of birds. Peregrine falcons were once known as duck hawks because they are quite adept at catching waterfowl. While peregrines mainly hunt small- to medium-sized birds, they can catch birds as large as geese and herons. Some birds, such as starlings and shorebirds, fly in tight flocks for protection because it is harder for peregrines to catch one bird with all of the others in the way. Prey birds also try to hide in trees or bushes to take cover from hunting peregrines.

◄ A peregrine falcon with its prey, a small duck called a bufflehead.

SIZE

Look at the photo at left. Can you tell which bird is Linda and which one is Steve? You may be surprised to know that Linda is the larger bird, the one on the left. While the nestlings were small, Linda usually stayed nearby to protect them and Steve did most of the hunting. He often brought food to her, which she then fed to the young.

Females are larger than males in many different bird-of-prey species. Females tend to do most of the brooding of the eggs and young, and they are often the most defensive parent at the nest. Males do most of the hunting for the family. They are smaller and more maneuverable, and can catch young songbirds that have just left their nests. When the chicks are older, the females begin hunting more and they focus on larger prey. That way the two parents have a larger selection of bird species available to them and they don't need to compete with each other as much as they would if they were always hunting birds of the same size.

▲ Steve (right) passing a prey item to Linda so she can feed the chicks.

A smaller male flying above a larger female.

▲ Linda delicately feeds one of her very young chicks.

FEEDING

When peregrines feed they first have to pluck away many of the prey's feathers. Feathers are not very nutritious, so eating them isn't worthwhile. Then they use their sharp beaks to tear small bits off of the prey to swallow. Peregrines usually eat on the ground, especially if the prey they kill is too heavy to fly off with. If the prey is small enough, they often carry it to an elevated perch. Sometimes they eat small prey in the air as they are flying.

When the chicks were very little, Linda and Steve had to rip their food into very small pieces and put each piece directly into a chick's mouth. As they got older, the chicks began to eat bigger pieces and eventually were able to rip pieces off of the prey themselves.

◂ Linda feeds her growing chicks.

GROWING

- The chicks are very helpless.
- Their eyes remain closed for the first couple of days after hatching.
- They are covered in fluffy white down.
- They need protection from the cold and rain.
- The female parent usually guards the chicks while the male hunts
- The chicks are fed small bits of food by their parents.

Luke, Joe, Katie and Refrigerator grew very quickly. By the time they can fly, peregrines may weigh twenty times more than they weighed when they first hatched. That would be the same as an eight-pound human baby growing into a 160-pound adult in only six weeks! Check out the chicks' milestones during their time in the nest.

The chicks are only a day or two old.

Steve brooding the chicks.

32

The chicks can now swallow bigger chunks of food.

The first chick to leave the flower box. Note its developing wing flight feathers.

WEEK 3 AND 4

- The chicks start to grow flight feathers and body feathers.
- They also start to flap their wings.
- They become better at moving around the nest.
- They can now swallow large chunks of food.

WEEK 5 AND 6

- There is much more wing flapping.
- The chicks' body feathers begin to develop and show.
- They can now tear meat off of carcasses by themselves.
- During the sixth week, most of the chicks will take their first full flight.

▶ At this point, the chicks begin to develop body feathers covering their downy feathers.

FEATHERS

The nestlings will eventually get a full set of feathers. There are three main types of feathers:

- **down feathers**, which are good for warmth;
- **body feathers**, which protect the body from rain and wind; and
- **flight feathers** (shown below), which are located on the wings and tail, and allow the bird to fly.

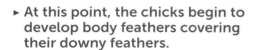

33

▼ Researchers are careful when approaching the chicks because the parents may believe that their chicks are in danger. The researchers wear helmets and hold brooms to protect themselves without harming Linda or Steve.

BANDING

A Connecticut warbler with band.

Because peregrine falcons have been on the endangered species list, researchers want to keep track of their numbers and learn as much as they can about the species. One way to do this is to band young peregrines before they leave their nests. Researchers attach a small band to a leg of each bird. Each band has a unique sequence of numbers so the individual bird can be identified from a distance. At four weeks of age, Linda and Steve's chicks were weighed, measured and banded by researchers. The researchers determined that Luke, Joe and Katie were females, so they were banded with blue bands. Refrigerator was the only male, so he got a red band.

Banding birds for scientific research has been happening for over 100 years. Most birds are banded with a metal band that has a unique number on it. When the bird is caught again, scientists can figure out how far it has traveled and how old it is. This research has allowed us to understand special migration routes and whether or not birds use the same summer or winter homes every year.

Katie gets her own special band.

◄ Dacey finally gets to hold one of his neighbors. Gloves are worn because even at a young age the chicks have very strong and sharp talons.

RESEARCH

Knowing the chicks as individuals can reveal a lot about peregrine falcons and how they raise their young. Here are some questions that researchers could ask:

- Do females grow faster than males?

- Is one of the chicks more dominant than the others and, if so, does it get more food from the parents?

- Do city chicks grow faster than natural cliff-edge chicks?

Imagine you were a research scientist. What questions would you ask?

RADIO TRANSMITTER

Some peregrine falcons get fitted with a special research tool in addition to their band: a radio transmitter. Radio transmitters allow researchers to use satellites to keep track of where a particular bird flies. The word "peregrine" means "wanderer," making it a great name for a bird that can migrate hundreds of miles away from where it hatches. Radio transmitters have shown that some American and Canadian peregrines travel all the way to South America in the winter and sometimes even migrate at night.

A researcher has just put a radio transmitter and antenna on this peregrine's back.

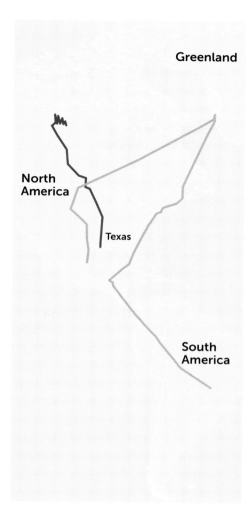

This map shows where two different peregrine falcons (one marked in blue, the other in gold) traveled after they were banded in Texas.

▸ What does Katie have to teach us?

◄ Luke is almost ready to leave the nest.

FLEDGING

ledging is the time in a bird's life when it leaves the nest and starts flying on its own. At approximately 6 weeks old, Katie, Luke, Joe and Refrigerator were ready for their first flight. This is a dangerous time for young peregrines because they aren't the greatest flyers yet, so they could easily hit a building or be caught by a predator.

Refrigerator (right) and one of his sisters sit on a new railing away from the nest.

Birds are more vulnerable when they stay in one spot to raise their young than when they sleep in normal roosting places. The nest site becomes more and more noticeable to predators as the birds' poop and leftover meals begin to pile up. So once young birds fledge from their nest, they usually don't return.

◄ **Look how messy peregrine nests can get!**

▲ One of the juveniles taking a pigeon from Linda.

TEACHING

Even though their chicks had finally left the nest, Linda and Steve weren't finished parenting them quite yet. The young peregrines, now called juveniles, are sort of like teenagers and they still need to learn how to hunt and take care of themselves. The adults help by bringing their young food as they learn their new skills.

Steve brings one of the juveniles some food.

KILL SKILLS

Young peregrines may stay with their parents for up to two months after they fledge. During this time, the parents may bring the juveniles food that isn't dead yet so the young birds can learn how to make a kill themselves. This skill helps them when they finally catch their first prey all on their own.

◄ The juveniles are now the same size as their parents, but they are browner overall and don't have the completely dark hood that their parents have.

▲ Katie and Refrigerator playing.

PLAY

Young peregrines need to perfect their hunting skills quickly to survive. One way they practice is by playing with their siblings. Katie, Luke, Joe and Refrigerator spent a lot of their time playing in the air once they learned to fly.

Many young animals play, including humans! Playing helps develop accuracy, coordination, endurance and social skills. Think about kittens pouncing on each other or chasing a ball of yarn; their actions are similar to those they will use when they jump on or chase prey as adults. When they play, juvenile peregrines learn how to stoop, chase, grab, turn and defend themselves, all while having fun with their siblings.

▲ A peregrine grabs its sibling's tail.

◄ Chasing each other is a favorite game.

ALL GROWN UP

Dacey felt like a proud uncle when the young peregrines left his balcony, all grown up. He is hoping that Linda and Steve might come back again someday to raise another family of chicks that will grow to become the fastest animals on Earth.

Steve and his prey come in for a landing.

Linda shakes off the rain.

Can you see the size difference between Refrigerator (right) and one of his sisters?

Steve with his sleepy chicks.

Steve tries to use a ▲
building to shelter himself
from a rain storm.

Linda with her ever-hungry brood.

One of the chicks getting big but still covered in
downy feathers.

INDEX

Note: Page numbers in bold refer to pictures.

PHOTO CREDITS

All photos by Luke Massey with the exception of the following:

p. 9: Shutterstock/ © Phoo Chan (top, left), Shutterstock/ © Don Mammoser (top, right), Shutterstock/ © FloridaStock (bottom, left), Shutterstock/ © Francis Bossé (bottom, right); p. 11: Ardea/ © Jim Zipp (top), Shutterstock/ © Tania Thomson (bottom, left), Shutterstock/ © Keneva Photography; p. 15: Shutterstock/ © YK; p. 17: Ardea/ © Steve Hopkin; p.19 © Mike Baird; p. 21: © Chris Earley (left), © NA (left); p. 23: Nature Picture Library/ © Andy Trowbridge; p. 25: Ardea/ © Auscape (top); Shutterstock/ © AEPhotographic (bottom); p. 27 FLPA/ © Michael Durham (top); © Brandon Holden (bottom); p. 35: © Chris Earley (top); p. 36: © Mike Yates; p. 39 Nature Picture Library/ © Shattil & Rozinski; p. 43 Nature Picture Library/ © Robin Chittenden.

The Publisher has made every reasonable attempt to properly credit photographs appearing in this book. In the event of an omission, please contact the Publisher for inclusion in subsequent editions of the book.